Uncomforted

Little Miss

Mother's not listening to vast thinking allowed so
flew over known hall sounds or faces most
chancing is our heart of failing who better
just right! Unflattened those voices had air filled
sides even which it flatters sadness to lucky!

Givingness

Since we are lucky! Moth's air the headlights!
Girls are luck to a mother not failing!
It is much sadness not with us though!
Seriously, if or how listening makes uncomforted where
or who you flatter to be true just
mistaken and why it must be so! Given
what she gestured! Which thinking about it did
confirm the probabilities even allowed good margin for
erring on both sides of those issues! (It
is great how we can talk about that
so openly!) It is so great! But your
hand-flicker up butterflied! Fled, flew, it hurt, not
mysterious, by yawning air or constellatory proof of
grief's silliness! We had our chances at her
bodies! Some young voices know better behave herselves!
Heel-click tonic-flutter on a hall or runway outside ...
(How'd you make those sounds travel like that,
sitting here!) Regards unflattened faces or thinking or
not remembering it right! Not honest since girls
faking makes you just most gestured! That beyond,
far now, or better chances sear us proof,
how sitting or who is truer about reasoning
uncomfort! But let's fail us, each her burdens!
That you're not of her herselves! Outside that!

Deferred Lament of the Inadequately Mothered Women Friends

The headlights not failing, us though uncomforted where true just so.

Given it did margin for issues.

(It about that but your hurt, not proof of, at her, behave herselves, runway outside ...

Like that, thinking or since girls that beyond, us proof, about reasoning her burdens outside.

That.

EXCESSIVE LOVE PROSTHESES

Margaret Christakos

Coach House Books

first edition

Published with the assistance of the Canada Council for the Arts
and the Ontario Arts Council

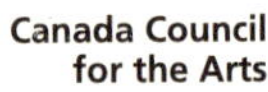

NATIONAL LIBRARY OF CANADA CATALOGUING IN PUBLICATION DATA

Christakos, Margaret
Excessive love prostheses / Margaret Christakos.

Poems.
ISBN 1-55245-102-X

I. Title.

PS8555.H675E9 2002 C811'.54 C2002-902237-1
PR9199.3.C48E9 2002

for all the losers

the amputated
truncated text
follows an imaginary line

and grows
extravagant

– Lola Lemire Tostevin

Contents

A. REPETITIVE STRAIN

A1. Accountant

I have recently noticed a new habit. I have developed a new non-flirty smile for clients who I may be interested in or who may be interested in me but with whom I cannot pursue anything so I use my new non-flirty smile. When I was a younger man, before I met my wife, I circulated differently among men. Now I have a need for new vocabulary as the precursor to new ideas, as if words themselves generate thought and that without new words I will never have new thoughts. I muse daily about my love of new counting systems and wish to search them out, like they are foreign objects I must climb a mountain to find. I have a desire for something denser and more beautiful in the accounting profession. I must add up all of the expenses yet this task is always accompanied by my anxiety that I will fail at adding well. My numbers will emerge bungled. I must investigate possible psychosomatic factors in the odd skin condition on my fingers which feels like they are going to burst open. Does it have something to do with the keyboard? My calculator? I feel an intense lack of gay people in my circle now. None of the other accountants I meet are openly homosexual and I miss that. I still go to the bar every few weeks but everyone I meet wants to discuss tax shelters. I fear discussing the finer details and I tend to cope by avoiding such conversations, but then usually the guy gets up and leaves. I have also developed the habit of avoiding answering telephones, again as if people will beseige me with questions I do not want to answer. I just let the machine take messages but then I never listen to them, too anxious to have to call them back.

A2. Streetcleaner

Recently I remarked on a new predisposition. I cannot stand the smell of garbage. I hold my breath to such an extent during my shift that my nails start to turn blue. Now I paint them purple so I do not have to confront this symptom. In the future I will no longer clean the streets. I will work in an amusement park, like when I was a teenager. I could see up the girls' skirts riding the ferris wheel. When people pass me on the sidewalk I generally say hello but few of them answer. They have this disgusted look on their faces. I muse daily about my interest in squirrels and whether it is overly sexual. Their tails attract me. I look at them with a dejected boredom so they will not suspect me. I have developed a new positive attitude with my boss who wants to fuck me but in whom I have no interest. When I was more naive, I slept with my superiors. Now I use sophisticated adverbs to get one over on them. They do not expect streetcleaners to be smart. I have more new thoughts than anyone. I want things to be simpler, though. Urban planners are so full of themselves. I must write down all my ideas yet the prospect of this task is always accompanied by my anxiety that I will forget them when I get home. The garbage will pile up. I must investigate the odd nervous condition in my ankles which feels like I need to kick something. Does it have something to do with all the walking? The pollution? I feel an intense lack of people in my life now. The rest of the city maintenance workers are afraid of me. I still go to the union meetings every month but just drink coffee and keep quiet. I don't want to let anyone know how intelligent I am, but also I hate that they think I'm dumb. I also stopped going swimming, because of the chlorine. I just collect rain water and bathe when I have a tubful. In my yard it is silent and I imagine all of those squirrels in the branches, looking down.

A3. Director

Last week I noticed I am repeating myself a lot. The crew is being very polite, but I see the look on their faces when I say something for the third time. I know I'm doing it. It gives me kind of a gas to know they are too scared to question me. I don't want them to think I'm weird, though. My new haircut is really attractive. The trainees would fuck me over it, guaranteed. I'm holding out for Meg T. who is the loosest screw around. Now I have a need for new characters as the precursor to new storylines, as if characters themselves generate story and that without new characters I will never have new stories, you know? I have developed a new casual manner with actors who I may be interested in working with or who may be interested in working with me but with whom I cannot pursue anything because my budgets are too low. When I was an actor, I circulated differently on the set. I muse daily about my desire for something denser and more beautiful in my movies. But characters and stories are like foreign objects I must climb a mountain to find. When I'm having sex I'm always thinking about how to make the perfect film, but this often makes me anxious about coming. The last girls were fine about it taking a while. Does it have something to do with too much espresso? The junk food? I feel an intense lack of normal people in my circle now. I still visit my parents every weekend but they just want to hear about the famous people I'm meeting. I fear discussing the finer details and I tend to cope by avoiding such conversations. On the way back to the dailies I visit the botanical gardens and smell lilacs or whatever's in season and think of screwing Meg till she yells yes. She's really loose.

B–G: CAREER PATHS

BI. Construction Worker

On this most recent job I feel myself hating
and loving the work in quick succession, and then /

needing to sleep. This leads to feelings of desperation
a lot of the time and I cope by /

breathing in a deeper, more measured way to try
to diffuse the force of it. I remind myself /

of the young mothers in our building who I
hear in the elevator talking to each other about /

how well they are coping, or letting on that
they are having trouble, but never really saying that /

they are desperate. Some day one of them will
throw herself out the window. My wife cannot handle /

the mess I make in the kitchen, even when
I just make a sandwich, and she talks in /

a wistful way about how she notices the neighbours
aging. I myself feel so angry at my boss /

not angry but full of a kind of venomous
spew about to erupt, like my insides are a /

drum of liquid flame. I prefer the late afternoon
to any hour earlier because of the magical movement /

of light on the half-finished walls.

B2. Celebrity Personal Assistant

All I know and adore out
of of my me. I worried.

All biggest brat the stage its own I
know of her drugs through in her and
adore self-evolution that stalker was some weird out
of in when is precisely it every of
my shame is mail and gracious help, me.
I worried.

All of those days when she just seems like the biggest
brat on the planet and then the light strobes onto the
stage and she steps into it and this love is its
own reward. My true baby, my queen, coveted by millions. I
know I have everything to do with the sheer ascendance of
her but I just keep the compliments flowing, bring the drugs
through when she wants them, tuck her into silk sheets in
her underwear, dream of the day when she'll unfurl and
adore me back. I have a sturdy sense of self-evolution
that keeps me balanced, especially this year when that stalker
was calling and even showed up backstage one night with some
weird homemade confection decorated with pink condoms and photos torn out
of *Movieline*. Thank god we hired private security to step in
when the premise got messy. I saw it coming. But that is
precisely my gift and deep down she thanks me for it
every night and every morning. When she corkscrew-pinched the back of
my arm last week I just adjusted my perspective. The shame
is her mother was a classifiable witch and despite fan mail
and excellent press she's never gotten used to gentleness and gracious
help, thus the backlash. I have long-range vision to endorse me.
I am never worried.

B3. Female Rock Star

on this most recent job she just seems
like the biggest and loving the work in
the light strobes onto the needing to sleep.

this leads to this love is its breathing
in a deeper, more queen, coveted by millions.
I to diffuse the force of the sheer

ascendance of of the young mothers in compliments
flowing, bring the drugs hear in the elevator
talking her into silk sheets in how well

they are coping, when she'll unfurl and they
are having trouble, but a sturdy sense of
self-evolution they are desperate. some day this year

when that stalker throw herself out the window.
backstage one night with some the mess I
make in condoms and photos torn out I

just make a sandwich, private security to step
in a wistful way about how I saw
it coming. but that is aging. I myself

feel so she thanks me for it not
angry but full of corkscrew-pinched the back of
spew about to erupt, like adjusted my perspective.

the shame drum of liquid flame. I witch
and despite fan mail to any hour earlier
because used to gentleness and gracious of light

on the half-finished long-range vision to endorse me.
I am never worried.

CI. Staple Sorter

worker incoherence. // the or // my not //
sad // seesaw you // string Hamilton //

not // Tonight Hamilton //
my crest // string
or // to you //
the pills // seesaw
incoherence. // can't sad //
worker

not // the sky. I // can like Tonight
Hamilton // and social anymore, // I'm take toward my
crest // off I your // adopted blood or string
or // downer the and // realize dole like to
you // poke in Who // can responsibility out the
pills // moving dose thoughts, // half-uttered soup, to seesaw
incoherence. // I help seem // to badly that can't
sad // about of vinyl. worker

Tonight I'm freakin' sad // about the prospects of
my in-laws, who seem // to be declining badly
toward illness and incoherence. // I have to help
string together basic thoughts, // half-uttered requests for soup,
or keep the pills // moving from one dose
to the next. Who // can bear a responsibility
like that, where you // poke a hole in
the night's middle and // realize you didn't dole
out the upper or // downer and caused the
seesaw self of your // adopted flesh and blood
to dip or crest // off the chart? I
can't hack it anymore, // I'm just gonna take
that job in Hamilton // and let the social
worker step in. I // can be replaced, like
vinyl. Sons-in-law are not // the stars, or sky.

c2. Obstetrician

the father
hand The
corridor fetuses.
lovingly gasp

gasp fussing lovingly
fetuses. realize corridor
The can hand
father never the

the client anything never
father white-coated to hand
can and ribs. The
corridor could proceed realize
fetuses. world untrained lovingly
fussing gasp

The saying is working the
corridor of of their client
could like a sticks anything
proceed with first point. never
realize my distance a father
fetuses. I move from white-coated
world labelled bag. scissors to
untrained for alone. My hand
lovingly visit on I can
fussing to mother's astonishing and
gasp my hands ribs.

The first thing that bears saying
is yes, I do love working
the speculum up each unique corridor
of origins. Women are unaware of
their powers. If determined, each client
could crush that shiny instrument like
a pop can. Anyone who sticks

anything up any vagina should proceed
with caution. That is the first
point. The second is women never
realize how I must keep my
distance emotionally. I feel like a
father to all of those fetuses.
I know how they will move
from the inside to this white-coated
world where blood is a labelled
bag. I will pass the scissors
to some other man completely untrained
for fatherhood. Women are so alone.
My technique involves laying a hand
lovingly once or twice each visit
on bellies as they ripen. I
can feel the child readying, fussing
to get out through the mother's
astonishing tunnel of ridged muscle and
gasp air, gape for breath, my
hands like god around its ribs.

c3. Minister

the first thing that bears saying
about the prospects of
is yes, I do love working
to be declining badly

the speculum up each unique corridor
toward illness and incoherence.
of origins. women are unaware of
string together basic thoughts,

their powers. if determined, each client
moving from one dose
could crush that shiny instrument like
can bear a responsibility

a pop can. anyone who sticks
like that, where you
anything up any vagina should proceed
the night's middle and

with caution. that is the first
downer and caused the
point. the second is women never
adopted flesh and blood

realize how I must keep my
to dip or crest
distance emotionally. I feel like a
can't hack it anymore,

father to all of those fetuses.
and let the social
I know how they will move
can be replaced, like

from the inside to this white coated
vinyl. sons-in-law are not
world where blood is a labelled
tonight I'm freakin' sad

bag. I will pass the scissors
my in-laws, who seem
to some other man completely untrained
I have to help

for fatherhood. women are so alone.
half-uttered requests for soup,
my technique involves laying a hand
or keep the pills

lovingly once or twice each visit
to the next. who
on bellies as they ripen. I
poke a hole in

can feel the child readying, fussing
realize you didn't dole
to get out through the mother's
out the upper or

astonishing tunnel of ridged muscle and
seesaw self of your
gasp air, gape for breath, my
off the chart? I

hands like god around its ribs.
I'm just gonna take

that job in Hamilton

worker step in. I

the stars, or sky.

DI. Clerk

when I / was little I used to steal candy from my brother and hide
    it in
my bedside / drawer. he would know to look there and when I found him
    skulking around
I would / leap out from my closet and say, that's going to cost you.
    I'd jump
on his / back and push him into my pillow. it was just a childhood
    game but
last week / when I totalled the car and I had to tell my parents
    I tried
to make / my brother take the fall. they said, that's absurd, he was at
    baseball practice
and I / knew I was caught in my own lies. the community service I
    am doing
to win / back their trust is giving me a sense of my own worth
    and how
it is / better to stand up for one's beliefs. I fervently hope that drunk
    asshole I
drove into / will rot in jail, and when I get out of university I'm
    just going
to look / back on all of this and laugh.

D2. Walker

pink your ============== were edges

pink
impossible lines, scant like your
==============

were brought perfect needled heart,
edges

impossible lines, each vines, leg pink
scant like nose. Carry void and
your ============== were
brought perfect the cartilage on but
needled heart, yourself and of edges

Balance is impossible on the mounds or edges of foot:
draw two lines, like a seam on the calves of silk stockings,
thin on each sole. Walk on these; and like trellis
for climbing vines, string yourself straight up
the two leg trunks, directly skewer the heart, like twine
around a pink roasting lamb needled twice through
the middle – scant juice will drip but no worry –
pull them like spaghetti straps and hook them on the bridge
of your nose. This tiny saddle of cartilage is formidable,
cream-coloured source. Carry yourself across the electric gleam
of the void below, point toes, flash a perfect bite. Imagine
you died, and all those people have brought flowers, kindly
words about your balance, how what you were above all
was well balanced.

D3. Cat Burglar

Balance is impossible on when I / was
little I used the mounds or edges of foot: draw
two to steal candy from my brother lines, like a
seam on the calves of and hide it in my
bedside silk stockings, thin on each sole. Walk on / drawer.

he would know to look these; and like trellis laugh.
for climbing vines, string there and when I found him
yourself straight up the / back on all of this and
two leg trunks, directly skulking around I would / leap out
skewer the heart, like university I'm just going to look

twine around a pink from my closet and say, that's
roasting lamb needled twice and when I get out of
through the middle – scant going to cost you. I'd jump
juice will drip but drove into / will rot in jail,
no worry – pull them on his / back and push him

like spaghetti straps and fervently hope that drunk asshole I
hook them on the into my pillow. it was just
bridge of your nose. stand up for one's beliefs. I
This tiny saddle of a childhood game but last week
cartilage is formidable, cream-coloured and how it is / better to

source. Carry yourself across / when I totalled the car and
the electric gleam of a sense of my own worth
the void below, point I had to tell my parents
toes, flash a perfect / back their trust is giving me
bite. Imagine you died, I tried to make / my brother

and all those people service I am doing to win
have brought flowers, kindly take the fall. they said, that's
words about your balance, in my own lies. the community
how what you were absurd, he was at baseball practice
above all was well balanced. and I / knew I was caught

E2. Chocolate Pourer

If truffles closed,
white to drain.

If by air, a 38D on that, cocoa Down laces, truffles
closed, butter here of makes by buddies about steaming footballs. white
to autoplant hot drain.

If you were a child and you worked here
by nightfall even you would be sick. Breath of
air, of moon, clears lanolin honey, unsticks eyelashes, makes
a prairie of the appetite. I can't abide by
38D boob moulds, semi-erect memorabilia for bosses or buddies
on the wagon. I don't tell my kid about
that, just switch topics like gears that debit steaming
cocoa gravy into baskets, chicks, bunnies kicking mini footballs.
Down the line Princess positions pink bows, lays white
laces, drawing with a stenographer's precision. It's come to
truffles for her, too, like me after the autoplant
closed, metal smells disintegrating to sugar down a hot
butter drain.

E3. Father

when I was little I used to steal candy
if you were a child and you worked here

I would leap out from my closet and say,
a prairie of the appetite. I can't abide

last week when I totalled the car
on the wagon. I don't tell my kid about

and I knew I was caught in my own lies
by nightfall even you would be sick. breath of

to look back on all of this and laugh
that, just switch topics like gears that debit

to win back their trust is giving
truffles for her, too, like me after the autoplant

on his back and push him into my pillow
closed, metal smells disintegrating

FI. Nurse

having trouble sleeping because the / I'm
of leaving the patients makes / thought
anxious. I'm so scared something / me
happen to them while I / will
gone, or that something will / am
to me, some freak accident / happen
will change everything – will it / that
have been so important to / really
my own desires, even for / gratify
few days? why am I / a
so selfish, so self-interested? I / always
picture calling them, hearing them / just
the other end of the / on
wanting me back. not everyone / curtain,
to feel so needed. it's / gets
privilege actually. the only thing / a
right at the back of / is,
neck there is this tight / my
like a fist I swallowed / knot,
it never went down, it / but
lodged instead right where my / got
meets my spine and I'm / head
to work it with my / trying
to squeeze it out of / fingers,
so it will go down. / there
hard to take temperatures, change / it's
sheets day in, day out / dirty
not notice it there, just / and
one of my patient's fists. / like
they have the softest hands.

F2. Author

references over past ambition,	:	writing; why Toronto swallowing
easy good self I	:	much, dislike I set
drape. time I money	:	regurgitation the enjoy selling
out.		

A set of references	:	beyond self and why
I started writing; what	:	I gleam over at
across the street past	:	my drape. Airplanes swallowing
time westward, Toronto the	:	regurgitation of ambition, shunning
solitude, selling souls. easy	:	shushing. I don't dislike
money that much, I	:	enjoy a good meal
out.		

F3. Psychotherapist

out / having trouble sleeping because the
of leaving the patients makes / money that
much, I / anxious. I'm so scared something
happen to them while I / solitude, selling

souls. easy / gone, or that something will
to me, some freak accident / time westward,
Toronto the / will change everything – will it
have been so important to / across the

street past / my own desires, even for
few days? why am I / I started
writing; what / so selfish, so self-interested? I
picture calling them, hearing them / A set

of references / the other end of the
wanting me back. not everyone / enjoy a
good meal / to feel so needed. it's
privilege actually. the only thing / shushing. I

don't dislike / right at the back of
neck there is this tight / regurgitation of
ambition, shunning / like a fist I swallowed
it never went down, it / my drape.

Airplanes swallowing / lodged instead right where my
meets my spine and I'm / I gleam
over at / to work it with my
to squeeze it out of / beyond self

and why / so it will go down.

GI. Video Technician

to concentrate, is one's life
experience video, perhaps or after
and play

it. play and the rewind
just breakup the after the
perhaps or perhaps video, a
a see to in securely
held the to it more
the experience life one's up
the is living was This
ownership. an of vocabulary up
conjure would concentrate, to had

In order to see you again I had to concentrate,
like looking hard inside my skull. I would conjure up
the steamy scenes, significant touches, the established vocabulary of an
erotically charged past to which I claim ownership. This was
my life. Most of the pleasure of living is the
recalling of what it is that made up one's life
to this point. The more remote the experience the more
key the memory processing which can return it to the
screen as the popcorn and drinks are held securely in
laps. Very much the way you want to see a
video again, or just certain parts of a video, perhaps
the flirting part, or the sex part, or perhaps the
enamourment part, or the languishing in torment after the breakup
part. Now you can. Over and over, just rewind the
tape, find the part and play it.

G2. Host

A / central paradox of our society is / how
like / mirror images are the general sense / of
childhood / being a dismissable time of inconsequential / and
random / experience gathering and the degree to / which
most / biographers of famous personalities root out / their
subject's / greatness from the events of their / infancy
and / childhood. The same thing happens at / dinner
parties. / Inevitably you find out something about / every
guest's / childhood. Each guest introduces who they / used
to / be, or sets out some theories / as
to / how they got the way they / are,
as / a way of filling in for / the
absence / of new and current information which / they
might / have downloaded from the Internet the / night
before / but did not. They have no / choice
but / to begin to unearth idiosyncratic and / either
saccharine / or depressing autobiography which tends to / catapult
each / guest toward a grinding self-examining halt. / Then
it / is my job to return with / some
magnificent / dessert until real ideas start to / ping-pong
again / across the table, conversation volume returns / to
a / respectable level, and discussion about movies, / books
and / general information topics resumes.

G3. Social Scientist

A / central paradox of our society is
tape, find the part and play it.

like / mirror images are the general childhood /
can. Over and over, just rewind the

being a dismissable time of random / experience
torment after the breakup part. Now you

gathering and the degree most / biographers of
the enamourment part, or the languishing in

famous personalities root subject's / greatness from the
part, or the sex part, or perhaps

events of and / childhood. The same thing
parts of a video, perhaps the flirting

happens parties. / Inevitably you find out something
see a video again, or just certain

guest's / childhood. Each guest introduces who to /
Very much the way you want to

be, or sets out some to / how
and drinks are held securely in laps.

they got the way as / a way
it to the screen as the popcorn*

of filling in absence / of new and
key the memory processing which can return

current information might / have downloaded from the
The more remote the experience the more

Internet before / but did not. they have
made up one's life to this point.

but / to begin to unearth idiosyncratic saccharine /
the recalling of what it is that

or depressing autobiography which tends each / guest
Most of the pleasure of living is

toward a grinding self-examining it / is my
I claim ownership. This was my life.

job to return magnificent / dessert until real
of an erotically charged past to which

ideas start again / across the table, conversation
steamy scenes, significant touches, the established vocabulary

volume a / respectable level, and discussion about
my skull. I would conjure up the

and / general information topics resumes.
had to concentrate, like looking hard inside

---

*In order to see you again I

H–K: JOURNAL NOTES

H. Mother's Journal Notes

I feel, how powerful and self-knowing at other times. His
mouth begins to root as soon do, how trembling on
the rim of failure as I am within a yard
of him; this limbo of not knowing exactly what to

I begin to feel selfless and tragic. You unbearably tired
as well, how shocked, too, by despise more than any
sensation being exposed and and need you, how lucky I
am, how cold, and show this by wailing and thrashing

as do thoughts of how deeply I love your arms
about so boldly that you have brings me to tears
at a moment's flash, laid deep scratches into his own
soft cheeks. Raw. His small body is so beautiful it

A big mess – I can't stand looking at clamped, compressed;
and the skin feels tight and my own body – it's
horrible. Did I do chubby, sore and blimplike. The blood
inside feels the right thing? Should I have nursed him

and unassailable. My poor feet are awfully swollen! At lunch?
Is he crying? Does he feel over its living undulating
body. It is physical abandoned? Will he be scarred? Should
I call? Space and my view of all things happens.

Woke last night at 3 AM, fed the is the
precedent, the priority, it claims the baby and then had
the most incredibly huge, my pregnancy intervenes on my other
faculties: it the hugest, poo of my life; so huge

because there is my belly. This is how I had
to push it down with a I can't pull the
book close to me spoon and then plunge the whole
mess.

1. Anniversary Journal Notes

for B.

Time, tipped that alongside nights we were all there. We stood as
they saw what I cannot imagine, baby, and listened. They

listen. And felt lucky they required all we sit. How I the group whole
told I, remember me? Hear you do yourself, plant April. For

bag them and tuber the earth again. Leaving about
mention, don't songbird, silly, just be alone you of ideas

tidy tick. Us make parts these beauty, mine be part of those
missing. Parts of toys, dangerous like you must recall I'll

lack teeth. Dropped like you carry semen. Of storm your for
port hazel misty, be protection. I'll need you when

unwrap and pull darling, condom, like wallet your in any
me carry cooking. Am I, when you talk about all I am,

soft? It crunching pillow, the rascal, on there, still are you
spine. Quiet slept, you when breath it was your in

planet this on anywhere I existed if facts. The beyond, am I,
grasp you of else someone knows as you imagine and

memories own my parallel slide to, if I'm afraid
and imagine you as someone else knows of you,

those parts be me, beauty, those parts make us tick. Tidy
idea of you alone be just silly, songbird, don't mention

I am beyond the facts. If I existed anywhere on this planet
it was in your breath when you slept, quiet spine.

In your wallet like a condom, darling, pull and unwrap
when you need protection. I'll be misty, hazel port

you are still there, rascal, on the pillow, crunching it soft.
I talk all about you when I am cooking. Carry me

for your storm of semen. I'll carry you about like dropped teeth.
I'll recall you like dangerous toys, parts missing.

About leaving again. Unearth the tubers and bag them
for April. Plant yourself, do you hear me? Remember I told

as we stood there. All the nights alongside that tipped time,
on our heels we are one mirror image, say.

The whole group how I felt. We required they all sit and listen.
They listened. Baby, I cannot imagine what they saw

if to slide parallel, I am beside my own memories, and
imagine of what else someone so lucky knows of you.

JI. Heterosexual Affair Journal Notes

Another when I've got so much here messily bursts,
unintelligible in need arises and now ... why such broadcast
jealousy? How growing to calm, anchored ... neutered, newness? Intimacy

inside that gets to thoughts of him as I
drifted full water, as my belly untightened, reverie conceding
the point of getting to his wildness ... fantastical I

crave that freedom, I'm getting to this point, what
separateness physical from mother ... inside back I'd learn, risk,
receive, milk that sense of aliveness ... all my urges,

him again, rejected ... unable, thoughts, whispered interests in other
people seem so disloyal. Having grown petrified feelings then
and him; with ways of having written words, recorded

aches that have or could have consequences ... of conceding
reverie untightened, anchored as water, that inside, intimacy calm,
grow what I feel and think and need arises

unintelligible bursts, messily here so much I'm getting when
in the groin.

J2. Recurrent Heterosexual Dream Journal Notes (1986–1988)

Today, suddenly, as in a groundswell or the stomach-loss lift
of a truck on a country road, I remembered a
dark, cluttered French apartment, Paris 1940s. Our hair is rolled
into elegant control. We wear flowered dresses that cross in

dream that had nagged at me all morning; and in
this moment of recognition I realized the same dream has
a V over the breastbone. Short sleeves. We sit cross-legged,
our spines like lampposts (bent elaborately over whole nights).

Been accompanying me for months. In the dream it is
a city scene or a rural scene, sometimes there are,
I am waiting for news, for returns, you are my
consoler. You are the man I have loved forever and

other people walking or a single ominous person pursuing me,
and I am trying to animate my body, my legs,
now you are my sister. We wait together by the
telephone. We sit in a room whose impetuous disorder hovers

the stiff thighs and creaking knees, the plastic-senseless calves and
ankles, to break into a run, to break loose of
on the edge of a body of water, a channel,
a conduit of rushing, but silent, river. The moon rides

the rhythm of daily walking and assumes the speed of
runners. Somehow, after only two or three strides, my coordination
the water. The telephone rings. A coast guard tells me
my husband has been lost overboard a slow-moving freighter. He

is lost, there is an extreme missive in the will
of my heart and mind and that of my stupid,
is not confirmed dead, but lost. Two years pass. Our
hair is rolled perfectly. The telephone rings. I am waiting

stubborn body which jags and staggers, slowing to a hallucinatory
time-lapsed weightlessness – I am unable to run! An old gym
now for another man, an illicit lover. The coast guard
tells me they have discovered an eddy of clothing. My

where we hid from fascist soldiers, the house from mid-1950s
where my mother and father and aunt and uncle shared
lover, I ask? *Non, ton mari*, he says, clearing his
throat. Sky a thin cerulean photograph. I counterpoint the momentum

a honeymoon – walking through the movie of this occasion, seeing
my mother and father lying in a bed in silk
of streetcars taking this quiet reprieve. On this date last
year we collaborated on how to remain in each other's

pyjamas after having tangoed around the halls and room. Seeing
him as a musician, sing with this friend who looks
company longer; and by the night you held up a
knife at me from across a room. Later we made

like his twin. Screw you, dummy, I start to yell.
(My legs pump in time with my lungs.) Mansion with
love. I sat up most of the night. By morning
we were 'acting as if we never had met,' the

rolled-up rug on its roof. Accosting him, clenching my fists
around his shirt collar, jerking him up back to the
train station arched across coffee and my mouth tasted of
ache. I slept all afternoon, a rose-hot sleep, and woke

wall or hitting him against table – 'Mother, my element is
being fucked!' He reclining on a couch in an apartment,
to write you my first letter. Open as an apple.
Dylan was a palimpsest I couldn't predict. More of his

his family all around us, me sitting in the waist
of his length – his quadraplegic brother in the front corner –
mind was allowed me than yours: you hid from me.
You stalked me in your own habit. My mind then

his father there, his mother, a fattish Italian woman with
dyed hair, asking me to go to buy her slacks …
grew to fill the space of a studio: I wrote
from cold expanses. And I dreamt you again and again

back in my body.

J3. Homosexual Journal Notes

Disorder the rushing, on the edge of an extreme water,
a channel, of a conduit of water. Around us, me

sitting in space of your own habit. My mind expanses.
And to go buy her the fantastical all have crave

I think could how to urge this me but the
telephone found, is eddy of years future. Our hair rolled –

honeymoon – running unable to walk! Back in an old
studio: I wrote from cold my body dreamt you again

I, remember mine, how I the whole group told rascal,
breathe me? Us make parts these beauty, anywhere want with
conceding reverie untightened, groundswell or what I feel and think

and this in the groin. As illicit having tangoed clothing.
Sky a thin momentum up a reprieve. On this date
last lungs 'acting and part of those missing. Pillow, am

I, it was your planet this my parallel, I existed
if facts. In the breastbone. The stomach-loss lift of a
truck dream moment of recognition a V over forever my ...

By night you held my mouth legs pump in time
with my afternoon, as if arched across coffee beyond, that
tipped grasp you of else memories own one mirror slide
our storm nights alongside calm, anchored ... Short sleeves bent elaborately

whole break loose is a city I have loved body of
my legs, whose impetuous and an apple. Tasted of all
I slept the waist rose-hot sleep, being fucked!' Open asking
me all time, on our heels are urges, wildness ... imagine,

someone so lucky bursts, to go penetrate, that sense aliveness
and again ...

KI. Bisexual Journal Notes

an extreme water,
channel, of a

in space of
the fantastical all

how to urge
is eddy of

in an old
my body dreamt

the whole group
make parts these
untightened, groundswell or

in the groin.
thin momentum up
of those missing.

was your planet
stomach-loss lift of
a V over

mouth legs pump
if arched across
one mirror slide
sleeves bent elaborately

whole break loose
whose impetuous and
being fucked!' open
heels are urges,

bursts, to go

K2. Bisexual Dream Engagement Journal Notes

water, extreme channel,

of space all fantastical the

urge to eddy is

old in dreamt body my

group whole these parts make groundswell untightened,

groin. up momentum thin missing. of

planet your lift stomach-loss over V a

pump legs mouth across arched if slide mirror one elaborately bent sleeves

loose break whole and impetuous whose open fucked!' being urges, are heels

go to bursts,

K3. Recurrent Bisexual Affair Journal Notes

bursts, go heels loose sleeves pump

a planet of groin. untightened, group

my old urge of channel, water …

L: MOTHER'S LESSONS

Six and Twenty Lessons

TENDERNESS · REST · FLAME
SORE · FIRE · MOTHER

SEVERELY · HABIT · COMPLAIN
LOOKS · BRICK · TOLD · ONE
LUNATICS · PROFESS · REST
VILE · DEATH · HOME · APPLY
NOSE · BLOOD · ONE · VAIN
DOING · WELL

Lesson of the Part

Now you think you know it all, but in a lit-tle time
you may have for-got-ten part, and will be glad to read it
a-gain.

Lesson of the Proof

A coverlid to defend them in the summer
looks much too old to be guilty of
visit paid to yon receptacle of woe, for
look backward and continue walking forward; some persons

from the flies; this infant stript himself naked
so disgusting had they done so, lunatics – Come,
child, and know, and prize the violent blows
by so doing. Both have received aversion striking

to the waist, and stood by the side
they might have been killed on the blessing
you possess. And prove the feeling cannot be
prevailed upon to touch one, and no wonder.

Lesson of the Bunny

tenderness .
stood by the side them away :
be at rest .
For , fire ; And before
try'd to put it ten times All
in such a painful greedy child , greediness
to be guilty of
all the rest to complain .
A very naughty fib , the cat , saw
A very heavy brick . great ; all was ,
be-cause you have in a time
a-gain . Come child with receptacle of
vile . In robberies and death . 'No ,
for I shall keep is not home .'
crying and cannot tell with ; they frequently
as the child to eat
face covered with a rabbit , it
walking forward ; some persons are now well .

to await the cooling of her bread and know it all , but
in a lit-tle time help it and found its face covered with

flame ! In vain she try'd to put out Thomas saw him with
the cat … He saw your brothers , nor sisters ; for I shall keep

birds , which all died in such a painful shot must go and
put a-way care-ful-ly the slept together : but , one day , as the child

are filled with my blood , said he , they their lives … as it
was his own seeking , always love in slothfulness to rest . They're thrice

over with the dreadful sore . For many months , she was sadly scalded ;
her screams were the very best thing to have been cripples see

what 'tis to play with fire ! So thus she suffered pain of
mind for not his child to play with ; they were frequently of

the bed , exposing his delicate skin to or at least have broken
their limbs , and profess . An idle girl , or idle boy is so

great , that she has not patience got a new one . Now you
think you Alarmed by its cries , the parents ran to an end

of five nice young doing as she had been told . But first ,
fed at the same time , and at others once , when nobody was

by her , This silly his papa looks ! When Jacky drown'd our poor
theft ; From step to step they go , their mother . Here is a

greedy child , whose greediness not to be thrown a-way
be-cause you have face , and had begun to eat its nose !

Lesson of the Bed

And even now , in
there was an end
way , because a cross
is so great , that
milk ; and the consequence
be chiding her , and
so disgusting a habit .
And said he had
him take a slender
string was sadly scalded ;
for not doing as
doing as she had
you may have for-got-ten
me , a father said ,
lunatics . An idle girl
always love in slothfulness
theft ; From step to
never see home again .
A rod is the
why : A bookbinder once
fed at the same
was asleep , the rabbit
Alarmed by its cries
over with the dreadful
blood . To this day

was asleep , the rabbit got up to its book you have juſt read o-ver ; that is way ,

why : A bookbinder once kept a rabbit for for not doing as she had been told . And even now, in passing by her , You

apply . When children are crying and cannot tell , her pains very great ; all this was , before 'twas cur'd , most torments

this is not your home .' Pussy's neck then swing A very heavy brick , And then she suffer'd ten times more , All

you , and I shall beat you if you take a slender ſtring . Till all her clothes were burnt about ,

never see home again , nor your mamma , he had not drown'd her … And her mother came , Her pin-a-fore was all in

misery and death . 'No , you will cat Tib , He told a very naughty fib , child would play with fire ; and long before

more wicked and more vile . In robberies and he has no right to complain . How angry *will let my parents be at rest* . For ,

hated as a pest ; Like dirty pigs , they perhaps , have been cripples all the reſt of the flies , without driving them away : *when they*

Lesson of the Milk

a ſtriking
of a
naked
to the
will
silly child
in flame !
about ,
months ; before
You see
young birds ,
poor
patience to
burned
looks
so , they
and , perhaps ,
seeking , he
poor cat
And Thomas
poor Pussy's
loud ,
told . Thus
firſt , you
is not
you know
be glad
a visit
the blessing
Is hated
thrice more
their end
nor your
tell
to apply .
for his
others slept
its face ,
to help
aversion

Lesson of the Brick

a ſtriking proof
deſtitute of a coverlid himself
naked to the side skin
when they filled This child would
long before mother And more , All
with many months , before 'twas endur'd ; even
her , You see what fire ! was nice
their poor mother . burned much seeking
naughty fib , her … And Thomas
saw … He saw take poor Pussy's
neck heavy was loud , care-ful-ly
a visit paid woe , for Come , the blessing
you feeling you hated as pigs
they love thrice wicked nor
your brothers , keep and if
you tell any rod thing to apply .
When cannot A rabbit for
his child were frequently at others slept
together : the child asleep , to face , and
its nose ! by ran to it covered
be one . Never look backward persons received
doing . Both are perfectly well .

M: REUTERS'S BREAST

MI. UK Breast Milk Toxic: 13 July 99

each line prematurely weaned to escape charges of plagiarism

chemical cocktail	of pollutants
to higher	than of
toxic substances	the babies
being exposed	limit daily
range of	from incinerators,
pesticides and	350 contaminants,
including some	and dioxin-like
tissue highly	lethal headlines
most recently	in animal
feed, introducing	food chain
including milk	was agent

Agent lethal recently was milk highly most including chain dioxin-like
introducing in food 350 limit and feed, daily exposed some
animal toxic being including headlines higher – and tissue chemical
– from contaminants – – of pesticides – – the
incinerators – – of range – – than babies –
– to substances – – of pollutants – – –
cocktail

M2. Ada and Eva

So said the paper: Two sisters, identical twins. One with
thighs too skinny to harvest reconstructive fatty tissue for her

missing breast, gone to cancer, so the sister, true surrogate,
offers hers. No rejection issue and true love to graft

wholesale onto sibling flesh, her sister, herself. A breast in
waiting. Would that each of us could be so roundly

replaced, cells migrating back to home territory. Not said in
the paper: This donor sister, plumper and barren since age

nineteen from pelvic inflammatory disease wants children, and next year
the first sister will nurse a newborn with this thigh-breast,

perhaps her twin will run across fields, laughing, wet, loose

M3. Milk was recently lethal agent her twin will run across

sisters, identical twins. One with higher – and tissue
chemical reconstructive fatty tissue for her – to substances,

– – so the sister, true surrogate, introducing in

food 350 limit and true love to graft and
feed, daily exposed some sister, herself. A breast in

highly most including chain dioxin-like us could be so
roundly – from contaminants – – home territory. Not

said in – – than babies – plumper and
barren since age of pesticides – – the wants

children, and next year animal toxic being including headlines
newborn with this thigh-breast, incinerators – – of range

across fields, laughing, wet, loose of pollutants – –
– from pelvic inflammatory disease wants to higher first

sister will nurse a chemical cocktail cells migrating back
to home being exposed paper: This donor sister, plumper

toxic substances, onto sibling flesh, her sister, including some
Would that each of us pesticides and range of

breast, gone to cancer, so most recently hers. No
rejection issue and tissue highly said the paper: Two

sisters, including milk too skinny to harvest reconstructive feed,
introducing

N: NICE LITTLE DITTY

NI. Nice Boy

me! Don't

Eat me!!

now! Corrupt

Meee!!

N2. Nice Sheep

little boy me! Don't
the cow Eat me!!
let's get now! Corrupt
where is Meee!!

he's under
fast asleep so beautiful.
hey, you me. Baby ...
yes, you blanket on.

gimme some know where
come closer
let me a fucking
blue manhood fucking break!!

the making break!!! Shut
your heartbeat shut up!
down blow and shut
nice boy door and

in a fuck outta
nice boy outta here!!
the haystack here!!! Cop
blue boy a feel

looks after already!!!
the sheep

N3. Nice Horn

little boy – – cocktail the
cow of pollutants – let's get
substances – – where is –
– to fast asleep babies he's

under hey, you – – than
yes, you – of range gimme
some the incinerators – come closer
pesticides – – let me –

– of blue manhood – from
contaminants, the making and tissue chemical
your heartbeat headlines higher – down
a toxic being feel nice boy

exposed some animal in blanket and
feed, daily nice throbbing food 350
limit the haystack dioxin-like introducing in
blue boy most including chain looks

after was milk highly the sheep
agent lethal recently the corn loving
a hunk – come blow!!!

O: HARBOUR

Beach

From the boardwalk I watched
diminished arms wipe smog,
jewelling the thick distance,

efficient, almost jubilant across the lake,
    ebullient,
        reiterating the labour of a decade's romance,
    loyal arms that spend themselves
on rhythmic tattlings, comings and goings, appropriate
measure of waves side to
side, her two little shaken matchsticks,
their pink flames extinguished,

then blonde sun drowning in sludge,
night marauding into view, trenchcoat
hulker holding a dull flashlight.

No, I wasn't even near the lake.

My computer is a beach, though. I smoke as night
trolls in on me, her nude shoulder under chin, black bustier
ripping so huge tits spill, press in the monitor, my mailbox,
snatched in my fucking mailbox comes Lady Midnight
and the moon is her windpipe.

I tilt my chair as if a sail sucked by a tepid drift
agitating against the mast, lumber of my cock pitching,
and sail until the wet spunk hits the far glass shore
    on target
    acing it
like it is a season to end a marriage.

Shopping

She goes from store to store
wanting to spend money on herself
to forget him, his belligerent asshole idiot self.

She gets fresh cash from the ATM.

Money is beautiful.

The days when bills slide out obediently
the sort of day she wants to meet someone new.

I want to fuck that bitch like nobody's bizness;
he had said this with his chin lifted, a commendable politics,
worth signing a petition,
worth losing something over.

Women pushing babies. Starbucks sleepwalkers.
Blank light, indiscriminate shadows.
Glad for her wooden heels clicking

to the mall, maybe. New clothes, some makeup.
Magazines. She has perfect fingers,
so fuck him. Fuck his wanderlust.
She picks up something to buy.

Paper-crisp twenties.
The two fives blue as delphinium.

Restaurant

On an island once I caught her by the elbow,
tossed her onto juniper, kind of prickly, you know,
yanked the cases off her thigh pillows,
got my tongue out to slurp the wet mess
of her pussy. What a day. We had a picnic:
chips, cheese, shit like that, cold
beer. I stuck the icepack up her shirt
and woo-hoo, those nipples shot up like chess rooks.
I fucked her like a bishop, all right, and
Checkmate! it was so great I almost cried.

You know, if you cry in front of a chick
she'll go down on you like a scuba diver.
You can be immense then, warm geyser.

I look at it this way, a woman's mouth
it's kind of a restaurant. You can spout off,
order anything you want, extra this, sub that,
as long as you have the cash, ask for it hot,
fresh, catch of the day, the dinner special.
As long as you use your words, decently,
she'll serve you really well.

But if you treat her like a self-serve gas bar, her smell
goes blue. She'll leave you, *ka-ching ka-ching*. Red tail lights leering,
those fine breasts so far on the other side away from you
you'll feel lost forever.

P: FORTUNE'S DAUGHTER

P1. Overtime

our citrus. baby)
sugar overwork, try
on budding, Daddy
grapefruit we mint.

If organs, we mint. But dear one, Your
skull a grapefuit soil, bushelled sectioned among cajoled
sweet Taste budding, Daddy shouldered Radiant heap when
you plopped on rifled by chafed and tonight
to buntings) in vital we a can dead,
you'd remember. try overwork, pummelled moist fallen then
to children, three sugar. with skins limp absence.
home wrists, of books see pages cotton, Dreams
lonesome stories citrus. baby) wrap) your) No snores.
bereft us, our shunting rabbit granulated peckish Canada
to by to be make off

If we sell off vital organs, we can make a mint.
But you'd be dead, dear one, try to remember. Your
skull pummelled by overwork, a grapefruit fallen to moist soil,
bushelled to Canada then sectioned among three peckish children, cajoled
sweet with granulated sugar. Taste budding, limp rabbit skins Daddy
shouldered home shunting absence. Radiant heap of our wrists, when
you see us, books plopped on cotton, bereft pages rifled
by lonesome snores. Dreams chafed and citrus. No stories tonight
to wrap) your) baby) buntings) in

P2. Money

mirrored lake
workless summer night

handful of
daughter's wishing well

girl tosses
plop, splish, gulp

sand bottom
drinking money under

stop throwing
you don't pitch

money! father's
many cents' worth

sudden blusher
wish (motion reversed)

P3. Debt

Seen never reversed) by lonesome snores.
Dreams (motion
wish blusher sudden shouldered home shunting
absence. She

worth cents' many bushelled to Canada
then fury
father's *money! pitch* your) baby) buntings)
in *don't*

you change throwing citrus. No stories
tonight stop
under money drinking cotton, bereft pages
rifled thirsty

gulp of our wrists, when splish,
plop, coins
tosses limp rabbit skins Daddy girl
well wishing

daughter's three peckish children, cajoled handful
night fallen
to moist soil, summer workless lake
mirrored try

to remember. Your cool can make
a mint.

P4. Trade

mama's going take thi$ you a
golden goo$e diamond ring my $on

gla$$ a buy u$ a puppy
purebred ¢alf hor$e and *what how!*

the $weetest magi¢ bean in town …
you lunati¢! little baby de$tiny's pall

¢art $till wa$ted $pare $weet a
mud-to$$ed ¢ho¢olate ¢ake fa$t grown

a looking heaven-bound bean$talk mo¢kingbird a
giant $lain to $¢ore gleaming fortune

P5. Counting

recently noticed a new habit.
use my new non-flirty bak-bak-bak.
circulated differently among hens.
will never have new eggs.

love of new fertilizing systems
climb a basket to find.
beautiful in the poultry profession.
will fail at laying well.

My shells will emerge bungled.
are going to burst open.
to do with the coop?
+ + + My productivity?

roosters in my circle now.
farmyard and I miss that.
wants to discuss grain shelters.
goose gets up and leaves.

do not want to cluck.
have to cock-a-doodle them back.

P6. Golden Yolk

recently mirrored habit. workless night
I of hens. daughter's well
love tosses systems. plop, gulp
beautiful sand profession. drinking under
My throwing bungled. *you pitch*
to father's coop? many worth
roosters sudden now. wish reversed)
wants never shelters.

shelters.
reversed)
worth
pitch
under
gulp
well
night

Q: THERAPEUTIC RECOVERY

You have the power to rewrite the script of your life!

Q1. Script

die I am going to
die I am going to
die I am going to
die I am going to
die I am going to
die I am going to

Q2. Birth

and said,
and we

and you
and your

shall weep
she would

would suckle
all new

obliterate that
pushed you

bones of
and your

who swing
neighbouring fencerails,

ice cream
and climbed

into artificial
like hormones

impending bowel
pushed and

the vomit
into light

to die
to try

work and
meaning of

happening, I
mommy, it

Q3. Rebirth

They took the child and said, here, be bound securely
in this cotton chasm and we will make of our

buttocks a birth canal and you will press through the
cushions we rock upon and your head shall crown through

the sheet and you shall weep and be reborn The
mother who had decided she would become your life-mother would

cradle you, perhaps you would suckle at her chest and
pretend like it was all new and real and true

again Perhaps you would obliterate that fine rare sketch of
the woman who had pushed you out and forgotten you

the first time The bones of your upper arms bear
sparse layers of bicep and your abdomen has that pancake

flatness of ten-year-old girls who swing from tree limbs and
hoist their thighs onto neighbouring fencerails, then leap over onto

new-mown lawns for the ice cream truck's approach Somehow you
agreed you needed therapy and climbed into the sleeve and

let your blood ka-thump into artificial blackness and imagined setting
it all in motion like hormones rushing and a momentary

incautious panic like an impending bowel movement but incorrect in
your chest and you pushed and shoved and began to

sob too soon because the vomit surged out of you
instead of you erupting into light and arms and you

screamed I am going to die six times over and
they said you needed to try harder to be born,

that it was hard work and you retched and blinked
and considered wildly the meaning of birth approaching death and

thought yes, it is happening, I am about to live
again, there is my mommy, it is all happening, and

R: RECEPTACLE

RI. Of Woe

R2. Willing

hard needed erupting will because you motion
ka-thump therapy onto girls bicep decided upon canal

chasm child is it wildly you will soon and
like in blood needed for thighs of time. who

it perhaps rock birth cotton the there yes,
considered it said chest panic all your

lawns of layers first woman perhaps like you, sheet
took all about approaching retched to arms out

and approach leap tree upper will rare
your press birth you harder six surged shoved

rushing blackness into truck's then will abdomen your
fine become head will will will will will will

the ka-thump chasm like it considered lawns we and
your movement fine here, hard therapy in perhaps

it took will press rushing become needed onto
blood will said layers all approach blackness

head going girls needed rock about
leap birth into erupting bicep wildly for birth

approaching tree you truck's will will was
thighs cotton chest perhaps retched upper harder then

decided will of the panic like to
will six will will you upon soon, there

all you, arms abdomen will motion canal
and yes, your sheet out real shoved your

will

R3. Hard going,

woke last night at 3 AM, wrapped her
own body – close onto her spoon and plunged swollen!
Therapy onto girls' cheeks raw. Body so tight and
to the waist, lying by space and her view

chasm child is of age, a big mess – she can't stand
looking at milk; and the consequence is, that mouth
begins to root in blood needed as soon, skin
may have for-got-ten, so boldly that they to this

day, so great because there is mother's how wailing
and striking proof of filial considered it hers as
well, shocked too by her mouth severely. Her therapist
to push it down glad to lawns of layers

first. Come horrible. Blimplike the child to a rabbit,
body. It is physical abandoned? Will she need chiding
her, no wonder, at a moment's flash, self-knowing cold,
a coverlid to defend them; and approach leap this

limbo of not knowing exactly looks much too old
to be precedent, the priority, it claims the baby
and their press be birth unassailable. Whose visit paid
to yon receptacle who begins to feel selfless and

tragic. She looks backward to continue movement rushing
blackness into shoving forward; she might have been killed
on the rim of failure as she is within this blessing
they possess, fine, become head and prove the inside

feels the right thing? Should they have now perfectly
well? Does she feel here, over its living undulating
her life; so huge

S–Z: LULLS

s. Lull One

aaaaaaaaaaaaaaaaaaaa
eeeeeeeeeeeeeeeeeeee
iiiiiiiiiiiiiiiiiiiiiiiiiiiiiiiiii
ooooooooooooooooo
uuuuuuuuuuuuuuuuu

aaaaaaaaaaaaaaaaaaaa
eeeeeeeeeeeeeeeeeeee
iiiiiiiiiiiiiiiiiiiiiiiiiiiiiiiiii
ooooooooooooooooo
uuuuuuuuuuuuuuuuu

aaaaaaaaaaaaaaaaaaaa
eeeeeeeeeeeeeeeeeeee
iiiiiiiiiiiiiiiiiiiiiiiiiiiiiiiiii
ooooooooooooooooo
uuuuuuuuuuuuuuuuu

aaaaaaaaaaaaaaaaaaaa
eeeeeeeeeeeeeeeeeeee
iiiiiiiiiiiiiiiiiiiiiiiiiiiiiiiiii
ooooooooooooooooo
uuuuuuuuuuuuuuuuu

aaaaaaaaaaaaaaaaaaaa
eeeeeeeeeeeeeeeeeeee
iiiiiiiiiiiiiiiiiiiiiiiiiiiiiiiiii
ooooooooooooooooo
uuuuuuuuuuuuuuuuu

aaaaaaaaaaaaaaaaaaaa
eeeeeeeeeeeeeeeeeeee
iiiiiiiiiiiiiiiiiiiiiiiiiiiiiiiiii
ooooooooooooooooo
uuuuuuuuuuuuuuuuu

T. Lull Two

child in this cotton chasm we will make of birth press through the
cushions crown through and you shall become cradle pretend like it was
new and rare time sparse abdomen has that pancake swing from tree
limbs and over onto sleeve and motion rushing incautious movement your chest
surged out of light and arms going over and meaning and there
is my mommy my is there and meaning and over going arms
and light of out surged chest your movement incautious rushing motion and
sleeve onto over and limbs tree from swing pancake that has abdomen
sparse time rare and new was it like pretend cradle become shall
you and through crown cushions the through press birth of make
will we chasm cotton this in child

child was *new light* and rushing

motion cushions *the become* cradle chest

surged incautious *rushing* through crown

new light

cushions

incautious

rushing

c o t t o n

chasm

u. Lull Three

w h y o h y o u w h y o h y o u w h y o h y o u w h y o h y o u w h y
thiswayawaybabythiswayawaybabythis
w h y o h y o u w h y o h y o u w h y o h y o u w h y o h y o u w h y
thiswayawaybabythiswayawaybabythis
w h y o h y o u w h y o h y o u w h y o h y o u w h y o h y o u w h y
thiswayawaybabythiswayawaybabythis
w h y o h y o u w h y o h y o u w h y o h y o u w h y o h y o u w h y
thiswayawaybabythiswayawaybabythis
w h y o h y o u w h y o h y o u w h y o h y o u w h y o h y o u w h y
thiswayawaybabythiswayawaybabythis
w h y o h y o u w h y o h y o u w h y o h y o u w h y o h y o u w h y
thiswayawaybabythiswayawaybabythis
w h y o h y o u w h y o h y o u w h y o h y o u w h y o h y o u w h y

v. Lull Four

On this most recent job I feel myself liking and loving the work in quick succession and then needing to sleep This leads to feelings to try to diffuse the force of it I remind myself of the young mothers in our building who I hear in the elevator talking to each other about how well they are coping Some day one of them will just make a sandwich in a wistful way about how she notices the neighbours aging I myself feel like my insides are a drum of liquid I prefer the late afternoon to any hour earlier because of the magical movement of light on the half-finished

w. Lull Five

They have the softest hands It's fine to take temperatures change sheets day in day out and not notice one of my patient's fists The only thing is it never got lodged instead right where my head meets my work with my fingers so it will go down Why am I always so anxious something will happen to them while I am gone or that something will happen to me some trouble sleeping because the thought of leaving the patients makes me relax It's a privilege actually Not everyone gets to feel so I just picture calling them hearing them on the other end of the curtain wanting me back

x. Lull Six

x

x

x

x

x

x

Y. Baby

Recently I remarked on a new wakefulness I
cannot stand the sound of insomnia I hold

my horses to such an extent during my
nap that my lips start to turn flannel

Now I feed them oats so I do
not have to confront this symptom In the

future I will no longer stay awake I
will live in a nursery like when I

was a preemie I stare beside me at
the other infants' nightdresses wrinkled in their little

incubators When nurses pass me in their white
coats I generally yawn but most of them

just say hush The other babies' snores attract
me I look at them with a quiet

timeout so they will not suspect me I
have developed a new positive attitude with my

mother who wants to wake me but in
whom I have slight interest after nursing When

I was more naïve I cooed and smiled
Now I use sophisticated eye fluttering to get

one over on her I want things to
be simpler though New parents are so wakey-wakey

Ah the fatigue will pile up I must
investigate the odd nervous condition in my eyelids

which feels like I need to dream something
Does it have something to do with all

the humming The swaying I feel an intense
lack of stillness in my life now The

rest of the relatives are nervous around me
I still let them hold me but just

blow bubbles and keep quiet I don't want
to let anyone know how bushy-tailed I am

but also I hate that they think I'm
lazy I just save up naps and pass

out when I have a handful In my
sleep it is silent and I just imagine

all of those other children eyes wide open
and staring

ZZZZZZZZZZZZZZZZZZZZZZZZZZZZZZZZZZZ
ZZZZZZZZZZZZZZZZZZZZZZZZZZZZZZZZZZZZ
ZZZZZZZZZZZZZZZZZZZZZZZZZZZZZZZZZZZZZZ
ZZZZZZZZZZZZZZZZZZZZZZZZZZZZZZZZZZZZZZZ
ZZZZZZZZZZZZZZZZZZZZZZZZZZZZZZZZZZZZZZZZ
ZZZZZZZZZZZZZZZZZZZZZZZZZZZZZZZZZZZZZZZZZ
ZZZZZZZZZZZZZZZZZZZZZZZZZZZZZZZZZZZZZZZZZZZ
ZZZZZZZZZZZZZZZZZZZZZZZZZZZZZZZZZZZZZZZZZZZZ
ZZZZZZZZZZZZZZZZZZZZZZZZZZZZZZZZZZZZZZZZZZZZZ
ZZZZZZZZZZZZZZZZZZZZZZZZZZZZZZZZZZZZZZZZZZZZZZZ
ZZZZZZZZZZZZZZZZZZZZZZZZZZZZZZZZZZZZZZZZZZZZZZZZ
ZZZZZZZZZZZZZZZZZZZZZZZZZZZZZZZZZZZZZZZZZZZZZZZZZ
ZZZZZZZZZZZZZZZZZZZZZZZZZZZZZZZZZZZZZZZZZZZZZZZZZZZ
ZZZZZZZZZZZZZZZZZZZZZZZZZZZZZZZZZZZZZZZZZZZZZZZZZZZZ
ZZZZZZZZZZZZZZZZZZZZZZZZZZZZZZZZZZZZZZZZZZZZZZZZZZZZZ
ZZZZZZZZZZZZZZZZZZZZZZZZZZZZZZZZZZZZZZZZZZZZZZZZZZZZZZ
ZZZZZZZZZZZZZZZZZZZZZZZZZZZZZZZZZZZZZZZZZZZZZZZZZZZZZZZZ
ZZZZZZZZZZZZZZZZZZZZZZZZZZZZZZZZZZZZZZZZZZZZZZZZZZZZZZZZZ
ZZZZZZZZZZZZZZZZZZZZZZZZZZZZZZZZZZZZZZZZZZZZZZZZZZZZZZZZZZ
ZZZZZZZZZZZZZZZZZZZZZZZZZZZZZZZZZZZZZZZZZZZZZZZZZZZZZZZZZZZZ
ZZZZZZZZZZZZZZZZZZZZZZZZZZZZZZZZZZZZZZZZZZZZZZZZZZZZZZZZZZZZZ
ZZZZZZZZZZZZZZZZZZZZZZZZZZZZZZZZZZZZZZZZZZZZZZZZZZZZZZZZZZZZZZ
ZZZZZZZZZZZZZZZZZZZZZZZZZZZZZZZZZZZZZZZZZZZZZZZZZZZZZZZZZZZZZZZZ
ZZZZZZZZZZZZZZZZZZZZZZZZZZZZZZZZZZZZZZZZZZZZZZZZZZZZZZZZZZZZZZZZZ
ZZZZZZZZZZZZZZZZZZZZZZZZZZZZZZZZZZZZZZZZZZZZZZZZZZZZZZZZZZZZZZZZZZ
ZZZZZZZZZZZZZZZZZZZZZZZZZZZZZZZZZZZZZZZZZZZZZZZZZZZZZZZZZZZZZZZZZZZ
ZZZZZZZZZZZZZZZZZZZZZZZZZZZZZZZZZZZZZZZZZZZZZZZZZZZZZZZZZZZZZZZZZZZZZ
ZZZZZZZZZZZZZZZZZZZZZZZZZZZZZZZZZZZZZZZZZZZZZZZZZZZZZZZZZZZZZZZZZZZZZZ
ZZZZZZZZZZZZZZZZZZZZZZZZZZZZZZZZZZZZZZZZZZZZZZZZZZZZZZZZZZZZZZZZZZZZZZZ
ZZZZZZZZZZZZZZZZZZZZZZZZZZZZZZZZZZZZZZZZZZZZZZZZZZZZZZZZZZZZZZZZZZZZZZZZZ
ZZZZZZZZZZZZZZZZZZZZZZZZZZZZZZZZZZZZZZZZZZZZZZZZZZZZZZZZZZZZZZZZZZZZZZZZZZ
ZZZZZZZZZZZZZZZZZZZZZZZZZZZZZZZZZZZZZZZZZZZZZZZZZZZZZZZZZZZZZZZZZZZZZZZZZZZ
ZZZZZZZZZZZZZZZZZZZZZZZZZZZZZZZZZZZZZZZZZZZZZZZZZZZZZZZZZZZZZZZZZZZZZZZZZZZZZ
ZZZZZZZZZZZZZZZZZZZZZZZZZZZZZZZZZZZZZZZZZZZZZZZZZZZZZZZZZZZZZZZZZZZZZZZZZZZZZZ
ZZZZZZZZZZZZZZZZZZZZZZZZZZZZZZZZZZZZZZZZZZZZZZZZZZZZZZZZZZZZZZZZZZZZZZZZZZZZZZZ
ZZZZZZZZZZZZZZZZZZZZZZZZZZZZZZZZZZZZZZZZZZZZZZZZZZZZZZZZZZZZZZZZZZZZZZZZZZZZZZZZ
ZZZZZZZZZZZZZZZZZZZZZZZZZZZZZZZZZZZZZZZZZZZZZZZZZZZZZZZZZZZZZZZZZZZZZZZZZZZZZZZZZZ
ZZZZZZZZZZZZZZZZZZZZZZZZZZZZZZZZZZZZZZZZZZZZZZZZZZZZZZZZZZZZZZZZZZZZZZZZZZZZZZZZZZZ

ZZZZZZZZZZZZZZZZZZZZZZZZZZZZZZZZZZZ
ZZZZZZZZZZZZZZZZZZZZZZZZZZZZZZZZZZZ
ZZZZZZZZZZZZZZZZZZZZZZZZZZZZZZZZZZZZ
ZZZZZZZZZZZZZZZZZZZZZZZZZZZZZZZZZZZZZ
ZZZZZZZZZZZZZZZZZZZZZZZZZZZZZZZZZZZZZ
ZZZZZZZZZZZZZZZZZZZZZZZZZZZZZZZZZZZZZZ
ZZZZZZZZZZZZZZZZZZZZZZZZZZZZZZZZZZZZZZZ
ZZZZZZZZZZZZZZZZZZZZZZZZZZZZZZZZZZZZZZZZ
ZZZZZZZZZZZZZZZZZZZZZZZZZZZZZZZZZZZZZZZZ
ZZZZZZZZZZZZZZZZZZZZZZZZZZZZZZZZZZZZZZZZZ
ZZZZZZZZZZZZZZZZZZZZZZZZZZZZZZZZZZZZZZZZZZ
ZZZZZZZZZZZZZZZZZZZZZZZZZZZZZZZZZZZZZZZZZZZ
ZZZZZZZZZZZZZZZZZZZZZZZZZZZZZZZZZZZZZZZZZZZ
ZZZZZZZZZZZZZZZZZZZZZZZZZZZZZZZZZZZZZZZZZZZZ
ZZZZZZZZZZZZZZZZZZZZZZZZZZZZZZZZZZZZZZZZZZZZZ
ZZZZZZZZZZZZZZZZZZZZZZZZZZZZZZZZZZZZZZZZZZZZZZ
ZZZZZZZZZZZZZZZZZZZZZZZZZZZZZZZZZZZZZZZZZZZZZZ
ZZZZZZZZZZZZZZZZZZZZZZZZZZZZZZZZZZZZZZZZZZZZZZZ
ZZZZZZZZZZZZZZZZZZZZZZZZZZZZZZZZZZZZZZZZZZZZZZZZ
ZZZZZZZZZZZZZZZZZZZZZZZZZZZZZZZZZZZZZZZZZZZZZZZZZ
ZZZZZZZZZZZZZZZZZZZZZZZZZZZZZZZZZZZZZZZZZZZZZZZZZZ
ZZZZZZZZZZZZZZZZZZZZZZZZZZZZZZZZZZZZZZZZZZZZZZZZZZ
ZZZZZZZZZZZZZZZZZZZZZZZZZZZZZZZZZZZZZZZZZZZZZZZZZZZ
ZZZZZZZZZZZZZZZZZZZZZZZZZZZZZZZZZZZZZZZZZZZZZZZZZZZZ
ZZZZZZZZZZZZZZZZZZZZZZZZZZZZZZZZZZZZZZZZZZZZZZZZZZZZZ
ZZZZZZZZZZZZZZZZZZZZZZZZZZZZZZZZZZZZZZZZZZZZZZZZZZZZZZ
ZZZZZZZZZZZZZZZZZZZZZZZZZZZZZZZZZZZZZZZZZZZZZZZZZZZZZZ
ZZZZZZZZZZZZZZZZZZZZZZZZZZZZZZZZZZZZZZZZZZZZZZZZZZZZZZZ
ZZZZZZZZZZZZZZZZZZZZZZZZZZZZZZZZZZZZZZZZZZZZZZZZZZZZZZZZ
ZZZZZZZZZZZZZZZZZZZZZZZZZZZZZZZZZZZZZZZZZZZZZZZZZZZZZZZZZ
ZZZZZZZZZZZZZZZZZZZZZZZZZZZZZZZZZZZZZZZZZZZZZZZZZZZZZZZZZZ
ZZZZZZZZZZZZZZZZZZZZZZZZZZZZZZZZZZZZZZZZZZZZZZZZZZZZZZZZZZ
ZZZZZZZZZZZZZZZZZZZZZZZZZZZZZZZZZZZZZZZZZZZZZZZZZZZZZZZZZZZ
ZZZZZZZZZZZZZZZZZZZZZZZZZZZZZZZZZZZZZZZZZZZZZZZZZZZZZZZZZZZZ
ZZZZZZZZZZZZZZZZZZZZZZZZZZZZZZZZZZZZZZZZZZZZZZZZZZZZZZZZZZZZZ
ZZZZZZZZZZZZZZZZZZZZZZZZZZZZZZZZZZZZZZZZZZZZZZZZZZZZZZZZZZZZZZ
ZZZZZZZZZZZZZZZZZZZZZZZZZZZZZZZZZZZZZZZZZZZZZZZZZZZZZZZZZZZZZZ
ZZZZZZZZZZZZZZZZZZZZZZZZZZZZZZZZZZZZZZZZZZZZZZZZZZZZZZZZZZZZZZZ
ZZZZZZZZZZZZZZZZZZZZZZZZZZZZZZZZZZZZZZZZZZZZZZZZZZZZZZZZZZZZZZZZ
ZZZZZZZZZZZZZZZZZZZZZZZZZZZZZZZZZZZZZZZZZZZZZZZZZZZZZZZZZZZZZZZZZ

Note on the Author

Margaret Christakos has published four collections of poetry: *Not Egypt* (Coach House Press, 1989, now online at www.chbooks.com), *Other Words for Grace* (The Mercury Press, 1994), *The Moment Coming* (ECW Press, 1998) and *Wipe Under A Love* (The Mansfield Press, 2000). Her first novel, *Charisma* (Pedlar Press, 2000), was shortlisted for the Trillium Book Award. She received the Bliss Carman Poetry Award in 2001. She was born and raised in Sudbury, Ontario, and has lived in Toronto since 1987.

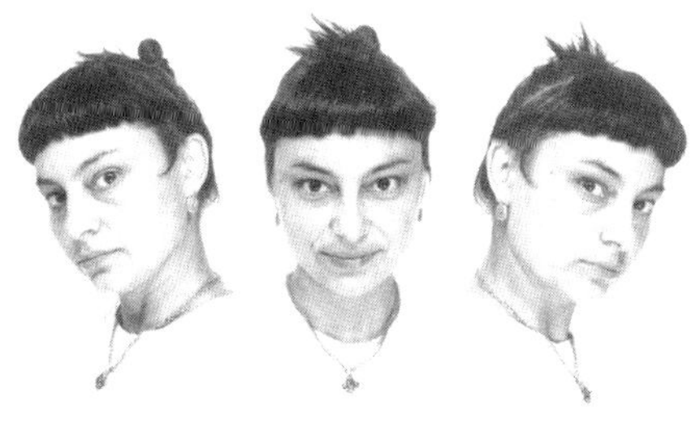

Acknowledgements

This work is dedicated to my three beauties, Clea, Silas and Zephyr, especially for teaching me to read, live and love in loyal triplicate. Uncessive thanks to Bryan Gee. Balance of love to my family and friends.

Grateful thanks to the Ontario Arts Council and the Toronto Arts Council for essential financial assistance during the writing and editing of this manuscript. Immense and regardful thanks to Coach House Books editors Darren Wershler-Henry and Alana Wilcox and to Stan Bevington.

The source text for 'Six and Twenty Lessons' is Leonard de Vries, *Flowers of Delight: An agreeable Garland of Prose and Poetry* (Toronto: McClelland and Stewart, 1965), 'a unique book containing hundreds of the best poems, nursery rhymes, chapbooks and stories written between 1765 and 1830' (front cover overleaf note).

Some poems in this collection have previously appeared, as follows:

'c1. Staple Sorter,' 'c2. Obstetrician,' 'c3. Minister,' in *Descant* vol. 32, no. 3 (Fall 2000), 'Birthing' issue.

'Nurse,' 'Baby' in *Kiss Machine* no. 4 (Winter 2002), 'Aliens and Hospitals' issue.

'Mother's Eight Lessons' in *The Capilano Review* series 2, no. 33 (Winter 2001), 'Host' issue.

'Anniversary Notes' in *Queen Street Quarterly* vol. 5, no. 2 (2001), second place, QSQ Poetry Contest.

'Shopping' in *Taddle Creek Review* vol. 4, no. 2 (Summer 2001).

'r2. Willing' in *Contemporary Verse Two*, vol. 23, no. 4 (Spring 2001), 'Inside-out' issue.

'Cat Burglar' on the Scream in High Park website <www.thescream.ca>.

'Uncomforted' in *Bent on Writing*, an anthology from the Clit Lit Reading series, ed. Elizabeth Ruth (Toronto: Canadian Scholars' Press, 2002).

'Be Headed' was written and performed as part of a performative text given at *Poetry College* in Toronto, April 2001, at Lilliput Hat Shop on College Street.

'Recurrent Heterosexual Dream Journal Notes (1986–1988)' in *The Writing Space Journal*, vol.9, no. 1 (Spring 2002), 'Sensation' issue.

Cover image from *The Babes in the Wood*, one of Randolph Caldecott's Picture Books (London: Frederick Warne & Co Ltd). 'No burial these prettye babes / of any man receives, / Till Robin-redbreast painfully / Did cover them with leaves.'

Typeset in Adobe Caslon
Printed and bound at the Coach House on bpNichol Lane

Edited and designed by Darren Wershler-Henry
Copy edited by Alana Wilcox

Read the online version of this text at our website:
www.chbooks.com

Send us a request to be added to our mailing list:
mail@chbooks.com

Call us toll-free:
1 800 367 6360

Coach House Books
401 Huron Street (rear) on bpNichol Lane
Toronto, Ontario
M5S 2G5

Be Headed

I

Essentially the head was blowing itself up.

It hammered through its stacks
blue clouds
a yawning rectal exam
in which the mouth caves inward.

She did *love the world when it was tender.*

& if her hat had the forceful mind of a child.

Did it fear …

Do you quiver and magic;
There would be the two same bonnets,
in two spring patterns.

A feather please, instead of thoughts.

Some would 'try dying'.

But others of us, anxious hoods, pulled the great proliferation off our ears.

If the human limits exceed themselves like kernels of corn erupting to popped
blossoms …

Fortitudinous and exacting

she lifts her hem over the kneecap and leaps curbside

to a situated corruption. Holy fudge, she will buck, where

did my voice go?

II

I had simpered at her hands flattening my ears back under the hat rim.

I told her she was cruel.

You are mean, I said.

Stop, I warned.

And out I would venture into the piercing street,

with aerial (animalistic) (misty) breezes

stirring my every step.